Introduction

Welcome to "Fearless: 10 Steps to Building Unbreakable Confidence." This book is your roadmap to transforming your life by cultivating unshakeable self-belief and inner strength. Whether you're facing self-doubt, fear, or simply looking to elevate your confidence to new heights, the steps outlined in this book will guide you on your journey.

Confidence is not something you're born with—it's something you build. Each chapter is designed to equip you with practical strategies and insights to help you develop a fearless mindset. You'll learn how to break free from limiting beliefs, embrace failure as a stepping stone to success, and harness the power of positive self-talk. By the end of this book, you'll be armed with the tools you need to face any challenge with confidence and resilience.

This isn't just about feeling good—it's about becoming the best version of yourself, ready to take on the world without hesitation. So, are you ready to become fearless? Let's get started.

Contents

Chapter 1: Understanding Confidence

Chapter 2: Identifying and Overcoming Limiting Beliefs

Chapter 3: Building a Positive Mindset

Chapter 4: Developing Emotional Resilience

Chapter 5: Mastering the Art of Communication

Chapter 6: Cultivating Self-Compassion

Chapter 7: Embracing Failure and Learning from It

Chapter 8: Setting Boundaries and Saying No

Chapter 9: Surrounding Yourself with Positive Influences

Chapter 10: Fearless: Turning Fear and Failure into Confidence

Conclusion: What will you achieve after reading the book

Chapter 1: Understanding Confidence

"Confidence comes not from always being right but from not fearing to be wrong." – Peter T. McIntyre

What Confidence Really Is

Confidence isn't just a feeling; it's an inner belief in your abilities and a willingness to take risks, even in the face of uncertainty. It's about trusting yourself and your potential, no matter what life throws your way. But here's something only 30% of people might know: confidence is closely linked to a specific area of your brain called the ventromedial prefrontal cortex (vmPFC). This part of the brain helps regulate emotional responses and plays a critical role in decision-making and self-perception. When you strengthen your confidence, you're actually rewiring your brain to respond more positively to challenges.

- Self-Perception: Confidence is rooted in how you view yourself. It's not about being perfect; it's about recognizing your strengths and acknowledging your worth.

- Resilience: True confidence allows you to bounce back from setbacks. It's the inner voice that tells you to keep going, even when things get tough.
- Courage: Confidence doesn't mean you're never afraid; it means you're willing to face your fears and take action anyway.

The Confidence Spectrum

Confidence isn't a one-size-fits-all trait. It exists on a spectrum, and understanding where you fall on that spectrum can help you tailor your approach to building unbreakable confidence.

- Overconfidence: Some people fall on the extreme end of the spectrum, where their confidence borders on arrogance. This can lead to reckless decisions and a refusal to acknowledge mistakes.
- Underconfidence: On the other end, underconfidence can hold you back from taking opportunities and risks that could lead to growth.
- Balanced Confidence: The sweet spot is a balance between the two. It's where you're aware of your abilities, but also open to learning and growth.

"The moment you doubt whether you can fly, you cease forever to be able to do it." – J.M. Barrie, Peter Pan

Confidence and the Subconscious Mind

Did you know that your subconscious mind plays a massive role in your confidence levels? About 95% of your thoughts, emotions, and decisions are influenced by your subconscious, which operates on autopilot based on past experiences and conditioning. By actively working on your confidence, you're reprogramming your subconscious to support your goals and aspirations.

- Positive Affirmations: Repeating positive affirmations isn't just a feel-good exercise—it's a method of rewiring your subconscious mind to reinforce your confidence.
- Visualization: When you visualize success, your brain interprets it as real, making it easier to achieve in reality. This is because the brain doesn't distinguish much between a vividly imagined experience and a real one.
- Mindset Shifts: Understanding that your mindset shapes your reality is key. Shifting from a fixed mindset (believing your abilities are static) to a growth mindset (believing you can develop your abilities) can significantly boost your confidence.

"Whether you think you can or think you can't, you're right." – Henry Ford

The Evolution of Confidence

Confidence has evolved with humanity. Early humans needed confidence to survive—whether it was hunting, defending their tribe, or exploring new territories. This primal need for confidence is still within us, and it can be harnessed to achieve modern-day goals.

- Evolutionary Psychology: Confidence was crucial for early humans in asserting dominance, securing mates, and protecting their communities. This ingrained trait still influences our behavior today.
- Cultural Influences: Different cultures have different standards and expectations for confidence. In some societies, humility is valued over assertiveness, while in others, boldness is celebrated. Understanding these cultural nuances can help you navigate social situations with greater ease and confidence.

"To be yourself in a world that is constantly trying to make you something else is the greatest accomplishment." – Ralph Waldo Emerson

Confidence in the Digital Age

We're living in an era where social media and constant connectivity can both boost and undermine our confidence. Here's something not everyone knows: studies show that excessive use of social media can lead to the "compare and despair" phenomenon, where you compare your life to the highlight reels of others, often leading to decreased self-esteem.

- Social Media Detox: Regular breaks from social media can help you reconnect with your own values and achievements, boosting your confidence.
- Curated Reality: Remember that what you see online is often a carefully curated version of reality. Comparing yourself to others on social media is like comparing your behind-the-scenes to someone else's highlight reel.
- Digital Boundaries: Setting boundaries for your online interactions can help you maintain a healthy self-image and protect your confidence.

"Comparison is the thief of joy." – Theodore Roosevelt

Chapter 2: The Power of Mindset

"Whether you think you can, or you think you can't—you're right." – Henry Ford

Understanding Mindset

Your mindset is the foundation of your confidence. It shapes how you perceive challenges, how you react to setbacks, and ultimately, how you view yourself. But here's something only 30% of people might realize: your mindset isn't fixed—it's malleable, like a muscle that you can strengthen over time. The concept of a "growth mindset" versus a "fixed mindset" was popularized by psychologist Carol Dweck, and it's a game-changer when it comes to building unbreakable confidence.

- Growth Mindset: Believing that your abilities and intelligence can be developed through dedication and hard work. This mindset creates a love for learning and resilience essential for great accomplishments.
- Fixed Mindset: Believing that your abilities and intelligence are static and cannot be changed. This

mindset can lead to avoiding challenges, giving up easily, and feeling threatened by the success of others.

"I am not a product of my circumstances. I am a product of my decisions." – Stephen R. Covey

The Science Behind Mindset

Did you know that adopting a growth mindset can actually rewire your brain? Neuroplasticity is the brain's ability to reorganize itself by forming new neural connections throughout life. When you challenge yourself, learn new things, and push beyond your comfort zone, you're literally changing the structure of your brain, making it easier to build confidence.

- Neuroplasticity: Engaging in new experiences and learning from them strengthens the neural pathways in your brain. This is why trying new things, even if they scare you, can boost your confidence.
- The Role of Dopamine: When you embrace a growth mindset and achieve small wins, your brain releases dopamine—a neurotransmitter that promotes feelings of pleasure and satisfaction. This positive reinforcement encourages you to keep pushing forward.
- Cognitive Reframing: By consistently reframing negative thoughts into positive ones, you can train your brain to default to a more confident mindset.

"Every strike brings me closer to the next home run." – Babe Ruth

Practical Steps to Develop a Growth Mindset

Building a growth mindset is about more than just positive thinking; it's about actionable strategies that shift your perspective and build your confidence over time.

- Embrace Challenges: View challenges as opportunities to grow rather than obstacles to fear. Each challenge you face is a chance to build your confidence and skills.
- Learn from Criticism: Constructive criticism is valuable feedback that can help you improve. Instead of taking it personally, use it as a tool to grow.
- Celebrate Effort, Not Just Results: Focus on the effort you put in rather than just the outcome. This encourages a growth mindset and helps you stay motivated even when things don't go as planned.
- Stay Curious: Cultivate a habit of asking questions and seeking out new information. Curiosity keeps your mind open and eager to learn, which is crucial for a growth mindset.

"In the middle of every difficulty lies opportunity." – Albert Einstein

Breaking Free from a Fixed Mindset

Many people don't realize how deeply ingrained a fixed mindset can be. It often shows up in subtle ways, like procrastination, fear of failure, or even perfectionism. Breaking free from these habits is essential to unlocking your full potential.

- Identify Limiting Beliefs: Start by identifying any limiting beliefs you hold about yourself. For example, thinking "I'm not good at public speaking" is a fixed mindset. Challenge that belief by exposing yourself to more speaking opportunities.
- Reframe Failures: Instead of seeing failures as evidence of your limitations, view them as learning experiences. Ask yourself, "What can I learn from this?" and "How can I improve?"
- Surround Yourself with Growth-Oriented People: Your environment plays a big role in shaping your mindset. Surround yourself with people who challenge and support your growth.

- Practice Self-Compassion: Be kind to yourself when things don't go as planned. Recognize that growth is a process, and setbacks are a natural part of it.

"It's not whether you get knocked down, it's whether you get up." – Vince Lombardi

Mindset in the Face of Adversity

One of the rare insights into confidence building is understanding the role of adversity. Did you know that some of the most successful people in history faced incredible challenges and setbacks? From Abraham Lincoln's repeated political failures to Oprah Winfrey's early life struggles, adversity often serves as a catalyst for developing a growth mindset.

- Resilience Through Adversity: Facing adversity forces you to adapt and grow. Each challenge you overcome strengthens your resilience and boosts your confidence.
- The Role of Grit: Grit, defined as passion and perseverance for long-term goals, is closely linked to a growth mindset. Developing grit can help you push through difficult times and stay committed to your goals.
- Embracing Failure: Understand that failure is not the opposite of success, but a part of it. Embracing failure as a learning tool can significantly enhance your growth mindset and confidence.

"Our greatest glory is not in never falling, but in rising every time we fall." – Confucius

Chapter 3: Overcoming Fear and Doubt

"Everything you've ever wanted is on the other side of fear." – George Addair

The Nature of Fear

Fear is one of the biggest obstacles to building confidence. But did you know that fear is actually a survival mechanism deeply rooted in our biology? The amygdala, a small, almond-shaped region in your brain, is responsible for triggering your fear responses. This was crucial for our ancestors, who needed to react quickly to threats in their environment. However, in modern times, this same response can hold you back from taking risks that lead to growth.

- Fight, Flight, or Freeze: These are the three natural responses to fear. Understanding how you typically react can help you develop strategies to overcome fear.

- Fear as a Signal: Rather than seeing fear as a barrier, consider it a signal that you're stepping out of your comfort zone. It's a sign that you're about to grow.
- Courage Over Comfort: The key to overcoming fear is choosing courage over comfort. This means facing your fears head-on rather than avoiding them.

"Do one thing every day that scares you." – Eleanor Roosevelt

Common Fears That Undermine Confidence

Identifying and understanding the specific fears that undermine your confidence is the first step to overcoming them. Here are some common fears that might be holding you back:

- Fear of Failure: This is perhaps the most common fear that holds people back. The idea of failing can be so paralyzing that it prevents you from even trying. But here's something not everyone knows: failure actually activates the dorsal anterior cingulate cortex (dACC), a part of your brain that helps you learn from your mistakes.
- Fear of Rejection: Whether it's in social situations, relationships, or professional settings, the fear of rejection can significantly undermine your confidence. This fear often stems from a deep-seated need for acceptance and validation.
- Fear of the Unknown: The uncertainty of the future can create anxiety and fear, making it difficult to take action. This fear is rooted in our need for control and predictability.

"I have not failed. I've just found 10,000 ways that won't work." – Thomas Edison

Strategies for Overcoming Fear

Overcoming fear is a process that requires patience, persistence, and a willingness to step out of your comfort zone. Here are some strategies to help you conquer your fears:

- Exposure Therapy: Gradually exposing yourself to the things you fear can help desensitize you to them. Start small and work your way up to bigger challenges.
- Reframing Fear: Change your perspective on fear by viewing it as a challenge rather than a threat. This mindset shift can make it easier to take risks and face your fears.
- Breathing Techniques: When fear strikes, your body goes into a state of heightened alert. Deep breathing exercises can help calm your nervous system and reduce the physical symptoms of fear.
- Visualization: Imagine yourself successfully overcoming the fear. Visualization can help you build confidence by creating a mental blueprint for success.

"You gain strength, courage, and confidence by every experience in which you really stop to look fear in the face." – Eleanor Roosevelt

The Role of Doubt in Confidence

Doubt often goes hand in hand with fear, undermining your self-belief and making it difficult to take action. However, here's a rare insight: doubt is actually a sign that you're pushing your boundaries and stepping into new territory. It's a natural part of growth and should be seen as an opportunity rather than a setback.

- Self-Doubt: Self-doubt is the internal voice that questions your abilities and worth. It often arises when you're about to take on a new challenge or step outside your comfort zone.
- Overcoming Imposter Syndrome: Imposter syndrome is a form of self-doubt where you feel like a fraud, despite

your achievements. Recognizing and challenging these thoughts is crucial for building confidence.
- Building Self-Efficacy: Self-efficacy is your belief in your ability to succeed in specific situations. By focusing on past successes and setting small, achievable goals, you can strengthen your self-efficacy and reduce doubt.

"Doubt kills more dreams than failure ever will." – Suzy Kassem

Turning Fear and Doubt into Confidence

The key to building unbreakable confidence lies in transforming your fears and doubts into fuel for growth. Here's how you can do it:

- Embrace Uncertainty: Understand that uncertainty is a natural part of life. Instead of fearing the unknown, embrace it as an opportunity for growth and adventure.
- Learn from Setbacks: When fear or doubt leads to a setback, use it as a learning experience. Analyze what went wrong, adjust your approach, and try again.
- Surround Yourself with Positivity: Your environment plays a significant role in shaping your confidence. Surround yourself with people who encourage and support your growth.
- Develop a Growth Mindset: As discussed in Chapter 2, a growth mindset is crucial for overcoming fear and doubt. By focusing on learning and improvement, you can reduce the power of fear and doubt over your life.

"Courage is resistance to fear, mastery of fear—not absence of fear." – Mark Twain

Chapter 4: Building Self-Belief

"Believe you can and you're halfway there." – Theodore Roosevelt

The Foundation of Self-Belief

Self-belief is the cornerstone of confidence. It's the unwavering trust in your abilities, decisions, and value as a person. But here's something only a few people might know: self-belief is not just a psychological concept—it's also influenced by your reticular activating system (RAS), a part of your brain that filters information based on what you focus on. When you consistently focus on positive beliefs about yourself, your RAS helps you notice opportunities and resources that align with those beliefs, reinforcing your confidence.

- Inner Dialogue: Your self-talk plays a crucial role in shaping your self-belief. Positive, encouraging thoughts

can strengthen your belief in yourself, while negative, critical thoughts can undermine it.
- Past Experiences: The experiences you've had throughout your life—both successes and failures—contribute to your self-belief. Reflecting on past successes can boost your confidence, while learning from failures can help you grow.
- External Validation: While self-belief should come from within, positive feedback and encouragement from others can reinforce your confidence, especially in the early stages of building it.

"I am the greatest. I said that even before I knew I was." – Muhammad Ali

Cultivating Self-Belief

Self-belief isn't something you're born with; it's something you cultivate over time. Here are some practical steps to help you build and maintain strong self-belief:

- Set Achievable Goals: Start by setting small, achievable goals that allow you to experience success. Each accomplishment, no matter how small, reinforces your belief in your abilities.
- Affirmations: Regularly affirm your strengths and potential. Statements like "I am capable," "I am worthy," and "I can handle anything that comes my way" can help reprogram your mind to believe in yourself.
- Visualization: Picture yourself succeeding in your goals. Visualization not only boosts your self-belief but also primes your brain to act in ways that align with your vision.
- Positive Self-Talk: Challenge negative thoughts and replace them with positive affirmations. For example, if you catch yourself thinking, "I can't do this," counter it with, "I am capable and ready to take on this challenge."

"You have within you right now, everything you need to deal with whatever the world can throw at you." – Brian Tracy

Overcoming Negative Influences

Even the most confident people face moments of doubt, especially when negative influences come into play. Here's how to overcome them:

- Identify Negative Influences: Recognize the sources of negativity in your life, whether they're people, environments, or even your own thoughts. Understanding where negativity comes from is the first step to overcoming it.
- Limit Exposure: Reduce your exposure to negative influences. This might mean distancing yourself from toxic people, avoiding environments that bring you down, or challenging negative thoughts as soon as they arise.
- Seek Positive Reinforcement: Surround yourself with people who uplift and support you. Seek out environments that inspire and energize you. Positive reinforcement from your surroundings can significantly boost your self-belief.
- Reframe Negative Thoughts: When you encounter negative thoughts, reframe them in a positive light. For example, instead of thinking, "I'll never be able to do this," try, "This is challenging, but I'm learning and growing every step of the way."

"The only limit to our realization of tomorrow is our doubts of today." – Franklin D. Roosevelt

The Role of Authenticity in Self-Belief

Authenticity is about being true to yourself—your values, beliefs, and desires. When you live authentically, your self-belief naturally strengthens because you're not trying to fit into someone else's mold. Here's a rare insight: studies show that people who live authentically experience lower levels of stress and higher levels of life satisfaction, both of which contribute to stronger self-belief.

- Align with Your Values: Take time to identify your core values—the principles that guide your decisions and actions. When your actions align with your values, you'll feel more confident and self-assured.
- Embrace Your Unique Qualities: Confidence comes from embracing what makes you unique. Celebrate your strengths and don't be afraid to let your true self shine, even if it means standing out from the crowd.
- Avoid Comparison: Comparing yourself to others undermines your authenticity and self-belief. Focus on your own journey and progress, rather than measuring yourself against others.

"To be yourself in a world that is constantly trying to make you something else is the greatest accomplishment." – Ralph Waldo Emerson

The Power of Self-Compassion

Self-compassion is the practice of being kind to yourself, especially in times of failure or difficulty. It's about treating yourself with the same care and understanding that you would offer to a friend. Here's something not widely known: practicing self-compassion can actually lower cortisol levels, reducing stress and allowing you to approach challenges with a clearer, more confident mindset.

- Practice Forgiveness: Forgive yourself for past mistakes and shortcomings. Understand that everyone makes mistakes, and each one is an opportunity to learn and grow.
- Encourage Yourself: When facing challenges, offer yourself words of encouragement. Remind yourself that

you're doing your best and that setbacks are a natural part of the journey.
- Be Patient: Building self-belief takes time. Be patient with yourself and recognize that growth is a gradual process. Celebrate your progress, no matter how small.

"You yourself, as much as anybody in the entire universe, deserve your love and affection." – Buddha

Chapter 5: Taking Action

"You miss 100% of the shots you don't take." – Wayne Gretzky

The Importance of Action

Confidence doesn't just come from positive thinking; it's built through action. When you take steps toward your goals, no matter how small, you prove to yourself that you're capable. But did you know that action also helps reduce anxiety? Taking action activates the prefrontal cortex, the part of your brain responsible for decision-making and planning, which helps to quiet the fear-driven amygdala.

- Action Beats Inaction: Even small actions can create a positive feedback loop, where success builds confidence, leading to more action, and so on.

- Progress Over Perfection: Waiting for the perfect moment often leads to procrastination. Focus on making progress, even if it's imperfect.
- Momentum: Taking consistent action builds momentum, making it easier to keep moving forward. Momentum is a powerful force that can propel you toward your goals.

"I like thinking big. If you're going to be thinking anything, you might as well think big." – Donald Trump

Overcoming the Fear of Taking Action

Fear of taking action is a common barrier to building confidence. Whether it's fear of failure, fear of judgment, or fear of the unknown, these fears can paralyze you. Here's how to overcome them:

- Start Small: Break down big goals into smaller, manageable tasks. This makes the action feel less overwhelming and more achievable.
- Embrace Discomfort: Taking action often means stepping out of your comfort zone. Embrace the discomfort as a sign that you're growing and pushing your limits.
- Visualize Success: Before taking action, visualize yourself succeeding. This mental rehearsal can boost your confidence and reduce anxiety.
- Set Deadlines: Deadlines create a sense of urgency that can push you to take action. Even self-imposed deadlines can be effective.

"I never lose. I either win or learn." – Nelson Mandela

The Power of Persistence

Persistence is the ability to keep going, even when the going gets tough. It's a key trait of successful people and a crucial component of confidence. What many people don't realize is that persistence isn't just about willpower; it's also about strategy and adaptability.

- Resilience: Persistence requires resilience—the ability to bounce back from setbacks. Resilient people see challenges as temporary and surmountable.
- Adaptability: Being persistent doesn't mean being stubborn. It's important to be flexible and willing to adjust your approach if something isn't working.
- Staying Motivated: Persistence often requires sustained motivation. Keep your goals in mind, and remind yourself why you started whenever you feel like giving up.

"The night is darkest just before the dawn. And I promise you, the dawn is coming." – Batman

Taking Calculated Risks

Confidence is often built through taking risks. However, not all risks are equal. Taking calculated risks—those that are carefully considered and weighed—can help you grow without putting you in unnecessary danger.

- Assess the Risk: Before taking a risk, assess the potential outcomes. What's the worst that could happen? What's the best that could happen? Weigh these against each other.
- Prepare for Challenges: Anticipate potential challenges and plan for how you'll handle them. This preparation can increase your confidence and reduce anxiety.
- Learn from Mistakes: If the risk doesn't pay off, view it as a learning opportunity. Analyze what went wrong and use that knowledge to make better decisions in the future.

"I don't have dreams, I have goals." – Harvey Specter

The Role of Discipline in Taking Action

Discipline is the bridge between goals and accomplishment. It's what keeps you moving forward, even when motivation wanes. Did you know that discipline is closely linked to your prefrontal cortex? This part of your brain is responsible for self-control and decision-making, and like a muscle, it gets stronger with use.

- Daily Habits: Establish daily habits that align with your goals. These habits create a routine that makes it easier to take consistent action.
- Accountability: Hold yourself accountable for your actions. Whether it's through a journal, a mentor, or a friend, accountability can keep you on track.
- Time Management: Effective time management is crucial for disciplined action. Prioritize tasks that move you closer to your goals and eliminate distractions.

"Discipline is the bridge between goals and accomplishment." – Jim Rohn

Chapter 6: Embracing Failure

"Success is not final, failure is not fatal: It is the courage to continue that counts." – Winston Churchill

The Fear of Failure

Failure is often seen as something to be avoided at all costs, but here's a rare insight: failure is actually one of the most powerful tools for building confidence. The key is to change your perception of failure from something negative to something necessary for growth. Did you know that experiencing failure triggers the release of dopamine in the brain when you eventually succeed? This means that overcoming failure makes future successes even more rewarding.

- Redefining Failure: Failure is not the opposite of success; it's part of the process. Each failure brings you one step closer to your goals.
- The Role of Ego: Often, the fear of failure is tied to the ego—the fear of looking bad in front of others.

Recognizing this can help you focus on the growth that comes from failure, rather than the temporary discomfort it may cause.
- Learning Opportunities: Every failure is a learning opportunity. Analyze what went wrong, identify the lessons, and use them to improve your future efforts.

"It's not who I am underneath, but what I do that defines me." – Batman

Famous Failures

Some of the world's most successful people have experienced significant failures. Understanding their stories can inspire you to embrace failure as a stepping stone to success:

- Thomas Edison: He famously said, "I have not failed. I've just found 10,000 ways that won't work." Edison's persistence through failure led to the invention of the light bulb.
- J.K. Rowling: Before her success with the Harry Potter series, Rowling faced numerous rejections from publishers. Her story is a testament to the power of resilience.
- Michael Jordan: Widely regarded as one of the greatest basketball players of all time, Jordan was cut from his high school basketball team. He used this failure as motivation to work harder and improve his game.

"I can accept failure, everyone fails at something. But I can't accept not trying." – Michael Jordan

The Benefits of Failure

Failure, while often painful, offers several benefits that contribute to long-term success and confidence:

- Resilience: Failure teaches resilience—the ability to bounce back from setbacks. Each time you recover from failure, you build mental and emotional strength.
- Innovation: Many innovations have arisen from failures. When things don't go as planned, it forces you to think creatively and explore new solutions.
- Humility: Failure keeps you humble and grounded. It reminds you that success is not guaranteed and that continuous effort and learning are required.
- Perspective: Failure provides valuable perspective. It helps you appreciate success more deeply and understand that setbacks are temporary.

"Failure is simply the opportunity to begin again, this time more intelligently." – Henry Ford

Overcoming the Stigma of Failure

Society often stigmatizes failure, making it difficult for people to embrace it. However, changing your mindset about failure can transform how you approach challenges:

- Normalize Failure: Understand that failure is a common and natural part of life. Everyone experiences it, and it's not something to be ashamed of.
- Share Your Failures: Talking openly about your failures can help reduce the stigma. When you share your struggles, it encourages others to do the same and creates a supportive environment.
- Celebrate Effort: Instead of focusing solely on outcomes, celebrate the effort you put in, regardless of the result. This shift in focus helps you stay motivated and resilient.

"Winners are not afraid of losing. But losers are. Failure is part of the process of success." – Robert Kiyosaki

Building Confidence Through Failure

The more you fail, the more opportunities you have to learn and grow. Here's how you can use failure to build unbreakable confidence:

- Fail Forward: Adopt the mindset of failing forward. This means viewing each failure as a step closer to your goals, rather than a setback.
- Track Your Progress: Keep a journal of your failures and the lessons you've learned from them. Reviewing your progress can help you see how far you've come.
- Seek Feedback: After a failure, seek feedback from others to gain new perspectives. Constructive criticism can provide valuable insights for improvement.
- Practice Self-Compassion: Be kind to yourself when you fail. Remember that failure is part of the learning process and doesn't define your worth.

"It's not about how hard you hit. It's about how hard you can get hit and keep moving forward." – Rocky Balboa

Chapter 7: Mastering Body Language

"Your body language shapes who you are." – Amy Cuddy

The Power of Non-Verbal Communication

Body language is a silent but powerful tool in building and projecting confidence. Studies reveal that over 70% of communication is non-verbal, meaning your body language often speaks louder than your words. But here's something only a few people know: certain power poses can actually increase testosterone levels and decrease cortisol levels, making you feel more confident almost instantly.

- Posture: Standing tall with your shoulders back not only makes you appear more confident, but it also signals to your brain that you are in control.
- Eye Contact: Maintaining eye contact shows that you are engaged, assertive, and confident. It also helps build trust and rapport with others.
- Facial Expressions: A relaxed, smiling face exudes warmth and confidence. Even when you don't feel confident, smiling can trick your brain into feeling more positive.

"Sometimes it's not about what you say, but how you say it." – Harvey Specter

Mirroring and Matching

Mirroring is the subtle art of mimicking another person's body language to create rapport. This technique is often used unconsciously, but mastering it can significantly improve your interactions:

- Builds Connection: When you mirror someone's body language, it creates a sense of similarity and connection, making the other person feel more comfortable around you.
- Enhances Communication: Mirroring can help you communicate more effectively, as it signals that you are in sync with the other person's feelings and intentions.
- Improves Negotiation: In negotiations, mirroring can make the other party feel understood and more likely to agree with your point of view.

"The way to get started is to quit talking and begin doing." – Walt Disney

Power Poses and Confidence

Certain body positions, known as power poses, can boost your confidence levels within minutes. These poses are all about taking up space and asserting dominance:

- The Wonder Woman Pose: Stand with your feet shoulder-width apart, hands on hips, and chest out. Hold this pose for two minutes to increase your sense of power and confidence.
- The Victory Pose: Raise your arms above your head in a V-shape, similar to how athletes celebrate a win. This pose can elevate your mood and boost your self-esteem.
- The CEO Pose: Sit with your feet on the desk and hands behind your head, leaning back in your chair.

This relaxed yet commanding posture exudes confidence.

"It's not who you are that holds you back, it's who you think you're not." – Denis Waitley

Understanding Microexpressions

Microexpressions are brief, involuntary facial expressions that reveal true emotions. Learning to read and control these expressions can give you an edge in social interactions:

- Spotting Deception: By recognizing microexpressions, you can detect when someone might be hiding something or not being entirely truthful.
- Building Empathy: Understanding microexpressions helps you connect with others on a deeper level, as you become more attuned to their genuine emotions.
- Self-Awareness: Being aware of your own microexpressions can help you manage your emotional responses, ensuring that your body language aligns with the image you want to project.

"The eyes are the window to your soul." – Traditional Proverb

Confident Gestures

Gestures can either reinforce your message or undermine it. To project confidence, be mindful of the following:

- Open Gestures: Use open, expansive gestures that take up space. Avoid crossing your arms, as this can make you appear defensive or closed off.
- Controlled Movements: Move with purpose and control. Avoid fidgeting, as it signals nervousness and insecurity.
- Handshakes: A firm handshake is a universal sign of confidence. Make sure your grip is strong but not

overpowering, and maintain eye contact as you shake hands.

"It's not the size of the dog in the fight, it's the size of the fight in the dog." – Mark Twain

The Importance of Practice

Mastering confident body language takes practice. Here's how you can improve:

- Mirror Exercises: Practice confident poses and gestures in front of a mirror. Observe how you move and adjust as needed to project confidence.
- Recording Yourself: Record yourself during conversations or presentations to analyze your body language. This can help you identify areas for improvement.
- Feedback: Ask trusted friends or colleagues for feedback on your body language. They may notice things you don't and can provide valuable insights.

"Act as if what you do makes a difference. It does." – William James

Chapter 8: The Power of Visualization

"What the mind can conceive and believe, it can achieve."
– Napoleon Hill

The Science Behind Visualization

Visualization is more than just daydreaming; it's a powerful mental practice backed by science. When you vividly imagine a scenario, your brain processes it as if it were real, activating the same neural pathways as actual experience. This is why top athletes, successful entrepreneurs, and high achievers use visualization to enhance their performance. Here's something not widely known: your brain can't distinguish between a vividly imagined experience and a real one. This means that regular visualization can actually help you build confidence and competence in any area of your life.

- Mental Rehearsal: Visualization acts as a mental rehearsal for real-life situations. Whether it's a job interview, a public speech, or a challenging conversation, imagining yourself succeeding can reduce anxiety and improve your actual performance.
- Neuroplasticity: Visualization enhances neuroplasticity, the brain's ability to reorganize itself by forming new neural connections. This makes it easier to learn new skills and adapt to new situations.
- Stress Reduction: Imagining positive outcomes can lower stress levels by reducing the brain's release of

cortisol, the stress hormone. This not only makes you feel better but also helps you approach challenges with a calmer, more focused mindset.

"Whether you think you can, or you think you can't— you're right." – Henry Ford

Creating a Vision Board

A vision board is a physical or digital collection of images, quotes, and symbols that represent your goals and aspirations. This tool helps to keep your goals top of mind and reinforces your commitment to achieving them:

- Select Your Goals: Choose specific, meaningful goals that you want to achieve. These can be short-term or long-term, but they should be clear and attainable.
- Gather Inspiration: Collect images, quotes, and symbols that represent your goals. These can be cut out from magazines, printed from the internet, or created digitally.
- Daily Visualization: Spend a few minutes each day looking at your vision board. Imagine yourself achieving each goal, and focus on the positive emotions associated with success.

"The only limit to our realization of tomorrow is our doubts of today." – Franklin D. Roosevelt

Visualizing Success

To harness the full power of visualization, follow these steps:

- Set the Scene: Find a quiet place where you won't be disturbed. Close your eyes and take a few deep breaths to relax your mind and body.
- Engage Your Senses: Vividly imagine the scenario in detail. What do you see, hear, feel, and even smell?

The more senses you involve, the more powerful the visualization.
- Focus on the Outcome: Picture yourself succeeding in your goal. How does it feel? What emotions do you experience? Allow yourself to fully immerse in the positive feelings of achievement.
- Repeat Regularly: The more you practice visualization, the more effective it becomes. Make it a daily habit to visualize your success.

"You must see it. You must believe it. And then you must never stop working to make it happen." – Arnold Schwarzenegger

Overcoming Visualization Challenges

Sometimes, it can be challenging to visualize success, especially if you're struggling with self-doubt or past failures. Here's how to overcome those challenges:

- Start Small: If visualizing big goals feels overwhelming, start with smaller, more achievable goals. As you build confidence, gradually expand your vision to include larger goals.
- Address Self-Doubt: If negative thoughts creep in during your visualization, acknowledge them, but don't dwell on them. Refocus on positive outcomes and remind yourself that you are capable.
- Use Affirmations: Combine visualization with positive affirmations. As you visualize, repeat affirmations that reinforce your confidence and belief in your abilities.

"Don't let the fear of losing be greater than the excitement of winning." – Robert Kiyosaki

The Role of Visualization in Long-Term Success

Visualization isn't just a tool for short-term success; it can also help you achieve long-term goals by keeping you focused and motivated:

- Goal Setting: Visualization helps you clarify your long-term goals and the steps needed to achieve them. By regularly visualizing your success, you strengthen your commitment to those goals.
- Motivation: When you visualize your future success, it creates a sense of excitement and anticipation that fuels your motivation. This can help you stay focused and driven, even when faced with obstacles.
- Resilience: Visualization can build resilience by helping you mentally prepare for challenges. By imagining how you'll overcome obstacles, you reduce the impact of setbacks and maintain your momentum.

"Success is the sum of small efforts, repeated day in and day out." – Robert Collier

Chapter 9: Surrounding Yourself with Positivity

"You are the average of the five people you spend the most time with." – Jim Rohn

The Impact of Your Environment

Your environment, including the people you surround yourself with, plays a critical role in shaping your confidence and mindset. Positive influences can uplift and motivate you, while negative ones can drain your energy and self-esteem. Interestingly, research suggests that emotions are contagious—surrounding yourself with positive, confident individuals can actually enhance your own confidence and happiness.

- Energy Exchange: Every interaction involves an exchange of energy. Positive people infuse you with energy and optimism, while negative people can sap your strength and bring you down.
- Mirror Neurons: Your brain contains mirror neurons that cause you to mimic the behaviors, attitudes, and emotions of those around you. This means that by surrounding yourself with confident, driven individuals, you're more likely to adopt those traits yourself.
- Social Influence: The beliefs and attitudes of your social circle can subtly influence your own. If you're around people who believe in their potential and take action towards their goals, you're more likely to do the same.

"Surround yourself only with people who are going to lift you higher." – Oprah Winfrey

Identifying Positive Influences

To build unbreakable confidence, it's crucial to identify the positive influences in your life and prioritize spending time with them:

- Supportive Friends and Family: These are the people who encourage you, believe in you, and celebrate your successes. They offer constructive feedback and help you stay focused on your goals.
- Mentors and Role Models: Mentors can provide guidance, support, and inspiration. Seek out individuals who have achieved the kind of success you aspire to and learn from their experiences.
- Like-Minded Communities: Joining groups or communities that share your interests and goals can provide a strong support network. These communities offer encouragement, accountability, and a sense of belonging.

"If you want to go fast, go alone. If you want to go far, go together." – African Proverb

Eliminating Negative Influences

Just as it's important to surround yourself with positivity, it's equally vital to distance yourself from negative influences that undermine your confidence:

- Toxic Relationships: Toxic individuals often belittle others, spread negativity, and drain your energy. It's essential to set boundaries with such people or, if necessary, distance yourself from them entirely.
- Negative Self-Talk: Sometimes, the most negative influence in your life is your own inner voice. Practice

self-compassion and challenge negative thoughts when they arise.
- Limiting Beliefs: Surround yourself with people who challenge limiting beliefs and encourage a growth mindset. Avoid those who reinforce negative thinking or doubt your potential.

"You can't change the people around you, but you can change the people you choose to be around." – Joshua Fields Millburn

Creating a Positive Environment

Beyond the people in your life, your physical environment also affects your confidence and mindset. Here are some ways to create a space that fosters positivity:

- Declutter: A cluttered space can lead to a cluttered mind. Organize your environment to create a calm, focused atmosphere.
- Inspiration: Fill your space with inspirational quotes, images, and objects that remind you of your goals and aspirations. Surround yourself with things that uplift and motivate you.
- Nature: Spending time in nature or bringing elements of nature into your space can reduce stress and improve your mood. Consider adding plants or taking regular walks outside.

"The environment you create determines the mindset you cultivate." – Unknown

Building a Supportive Network

To maintain and grow your confidence, it's essential to build a strong, supportive network. Here's how you can do that:

- Networking: Attend events, join online groups, and connect with like-minded individuals who share your interests and goals. Building a network of positive, driven people can provide you with valuable support and opportunities.
- Collaboration: Collaborate with others who share your goals. Working together towards a common purpose can boost your confidence and help you achieve more than you could alone.
- Continuous Learning: Surround yourself with people who value growth and learning. Engage in activities that challenge you and push you out of your comfort zone.

"Alone we can do so little; together we can do so much." – Helen Keller

Sustaining Positivity

Maintaining a positive environment and mindset requires ongoing effort. Here's how to sustain positivity in your life:

- Daily Gratitude: Practice gratitude daily by acknowledging the positive aspects of your life and the people who support you. This helps to reinforce a positive mindset.
- Positive Affirmations: Use positive affirmations to counteract negative thoughts and reinforce your confidence. Repeat them regularly, especially in challenging situations.
- Mindful Consumption: Be mindful of the media you consume. Choose content that inspires and uplifts you, and limit exposure to negative news or toxic social media.

"Happiness is not something ready made. It comes from your own actions." – Dalai Lama

Chapter 10: Embracing Fear and Failure

"Fear is a tool." – Batman, The Batman (2022)

Understanding Fear

Fear is a natural response to uncertainty and the unknown. It's designed to protect you from danger, but it can also hold you back from reaching your full potential. What many people don't realize is that fear can be a powerful tool when harnessed correctly. Fear is not just an obstacle; it's also a guide, pointing you toward areas of growth and opportunity.

- Fear as a Compass: Fear often arises when you're about to step outside your comfort zone. Instead of avoiding it, recognize that fear is a sign that you're on the verge of something important. It's a signal that growth is possible.
- Channeling Fear: Use fear to fuel your motivation. When you feel fear, instead of retreating, channel that energy into preparation and action. The more you face your fears, the more confident you become.
- Reframing Fear: Shift your perspective on fear. Instead of seeing it as something to avoid, view it as a challenge to overcome. This mindset change can turn fear into a powerful ally.

"Success is not final, failure is not fatal: It is the courage to continue that counts." – Winston Churchill

The Role of Failure in Success

Failure is often seen as something to be feared or avoided at all costs. However, the reality is that failure is an essential part of the journey to success. Here's a rare insight: most successful people have failed more times than the average person has even tried.

- Learning from Failure: Every failure is an opportunity to learn and grow. Analyze what went wrong, and use that knowledge to improve and try again. Failure teaches resilience and adaptability.
- Building Resilience: The more you fail, the more resilient you become. Each setback you overcome strengthens your ability to handle future challenges with confidence.
- Failure as a Stepping Stone: Failure is not the opposite of success; it's a part of it. Every failure brings you one step closer to achieving your goals. Embrace it as a necessary and valuable part of the process.

"The only thing we have to fear is fear itself." – Franklin D. Roosevelt

Facing Your Fears

To build unbreakable confidence, you must confront your fears head-on. Here's how you can do it:

- Identify Your Fears: Make a list of the things that scare you the most, whether it's public speaking, taking risks, or facing rejection. Acknowledging your fears is the first step toward overcoming them.
- Take Small Steps: Start by facing smaller fears before tackling larger ones. Gradual exposure helps you build confidence and desensitizes you to the fear over time.
- Visualize Success: Before confronting a fear, visualize yourself successfully overcoming it. Imagine the positive outcomes and how you'll feel once you've conquered it. This technique can reduce anxiety and boost your confidence.

"Courage is not the absence of fear, but the triumph over it." – Nelson Mandela

The Growth Mindset

Adopting a growth mindset is essential for embracing fear and failure. A growth mindset is the belief that your abilities and intelligence can be developed through hard work, dedication, and learning from experience.

- Embrace Challenges: See challenges as opportunities to grow, not as threats. When you encounter a difficult situation, approach it with curiosity and a willingness to learn.
- Celebrate Effort, Not Just Results: Focus on the effort you put in, rather than just the outcome. This shift in focus helps you appreciate the process and encourages persistence, even in the face of setbacks.
- Learn from Criticism: Constructive criticism is a valuable tool for growth. Instead of taking it personally, use it to identify areas for improvement and to refine your approach.

"I have not failed. I've just found 10,000 ways that won't work." – Thomas Edison

Turning Fear and Failure into Confidence

Fear and failure can be transformed into powerful catalysts for building confidence. Here's how:

- Fear as a Confidence Booster: Each time you face a fear and overcome it, your confidence grows. The more you challenge yourself, the more resilient and self-assured you become.
- Failure as Feedback: View failure as feedback, not as a reflection of your worth. Use it to make adjustments and improve, rather than letting it diminish your confidence.

- Persistence Pays Off: Confidence comes from knowing that you have the ability to keep going, no matter what. By embracing fear and failure, you build the mental toughness needed to persist through any challenge.

"Why do we fall? So we can learn to pick ourselves up." – Alfred Pennyworth, Batman Begins (2005)

Conclusion: Living Fearlessly

Embracing fear and failure is the final step in building unbreakable confidence. It's about understanding that fear is a natural part of growth and that failure is not the end, but rather a crucial step on the path to success. By facing your fears, learning from your failures, and adopting a growth mindset, you become fearless—not because you're never afraid, but because you refuse to let fear hold you back.

- Embrace Fear: Welcome fear as a sign that you're on the right path. Let it motivate you, not paralyze you.
- Learn from Failure: Use every failure as a stepping stone toward your goals. Each one brings you closer to success.
- Live Fearlessly: Confidence is not about never experiencing fear; it's about living fearlessly in the face of it. When you do, you unlock your true potential and become unstoppable.

"It's not who I am underneath, but what I do that defines me." – Batman, Batman Begins (2005)

What You Will Achieve After Reading The Book

By the time you've finished this book, your mindset and confidence levels will have undergone a profound transformation. Here's what you'll be able to achieve:

- Unshakeable Self-Belief:
    - You'll develop a deep, unwavering belief in your abilities.
    - Self-doubt will no longer hold you back—you'll face challenges head-on, knowing you can overcome them.
- Clear, Motivating Goals:
    - You'll learn how to set powerful, inspiring goals that drive you forward.
    - With a clear roadmap, you'll stay focused and motivated, even when the going gets tough.
- Mastery of Positive Self-Talk:
    - Your inner dialogue will become your biggest supporter, silencing negative thoughts.
    - You'll replace self-criticism with empowering affirmations that boost your confidence daily.
- Confident Body Language:
    - You'll carry yourself with a presence that commands respect and attention.
    - Even when you're not feeling confident, your body language will project strength and assurance.
- Resilience in the Face of Rejection:
    - Rejection will no longer sting—it will become a stepping stone to your success.

- - You'll learn to bounce back stronger from setbacks, turning rejection into valuable learning experiences.
- Overcoming Fear and Doubt:
  - Fear and doubt will no longer paralyze you. You'll face them with courage and determination.
  - You'll develop strategies to push through your fears, transforming them into fuel for your growth.
- Unbreakable Resilience:
  - Life's challenges won't knock you down. You'll develop the mental toughness to persevere through anything.
  - Resilience will become your superpower, enabling you to maintain confidence even in the face of adversity.
- A Positive, Supportive Network:
  - You'll surround yourself with people who uplift and empower you.
  - Toxic relationships will become a thing of the past, as you build a network that supports your confidence and growth.
- The Courage to Step Out of Your Comfort Zone:
  - You'll embrace risks and new experiences, knowing that growth happens outside your comfort zone.
  - Confidence will come naturally as you push your limits and achieve things you once thought were impossible.
- Fearless Mindset:
  - You'll learn to turn fear and failure into tools for building confidence.
  - By embracing fear and failure, you'll unlock your full potential and live life fearlessly.

www.ingramcontent.com/pod-product-compliance
Lightning Source LLC
Chambersburg PA
CBHW030058230526
45471CB00003B/1150